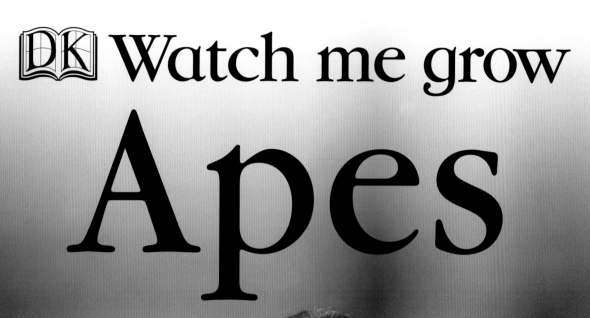

Watch me grow
Apes

LONDON, NEW YORK, MUNICH,
MELBOURNE, and DELHI

Written and edited by Lisa Magloff
Designed by Cathy Chesson
DTP designer Almudena Díaz
Picture researcher Marianna Sonnenberg
Production Lucy Baker

Publishing managers Susan Leonard
and Joanne Connor

First published in Great Britain in 2006 by
Dorling Kindersley Limited
80 Strand, London WC2R 0RL

A Penguin Company
08 09   10 9 8 7 6 5 4 3 2

Copyright © 2006 Dorling Kindersley Limited, London

A CIP catalogue record for this book
is available from the British Library.

All rights reserved. No part of this publication
may be reproduced, stored in a retrieval system,
or transmitted in any form or by any means,
electronic, mechanical, photocopying, recording,
or otherwise, without the prior written permission
of the copyright owner.

ISBN-13 978-1-40531-308-7
ISBN-10 1-4053-1308-0

Colour reproduction by
Media, Development and Printing, Ltd, Great Britain
Printed and bound in China by South China Printing Co. Ltd

Discover more at
www.dk.com

Contents

I'm an orang-utan

I was born in a green, leafy jungle. My mum and I live up in the trees. I hang on tight to my mother while she swings from tree to tree.

Hold on tight.

The baby will stay with its mother for about eight years.

4

Orang-utans learn to climb when they are around three years old.

We're just hanging around.

Fruit for breakfast

This orang-utan is eating a jungle fruit called a durian. Orangutans love to eat fruit, but they also eat leaves, bark, flowers, and insects.

Learning to climb

I'm three years old. My brothers and sisters are teaching me how to climb trees on my own, but I am careful to stay close to Mum.

Orang-utans have very strong hands and feet.

Hey – look at me, I can climb!

Orang-utan teeth are designed for eating fruit.

· ·

One adult orang-utan is about as strong as eight adult humans.

The arms of an adult orang-utan can be more than 2.5 m (7 ft) long when stretched out.

Orang-utans use many tools.

Be careful, little brother!

Family life

Orang-utans live with their mums until they are about 10 years old, when they go off to live on their own.

I'm a gorilla

I live with my family in a big forest. I'm only four months old and I can't walk yet so I hang on to my mum. I cling to Mum's fur while she looks for some tasty food to eat.

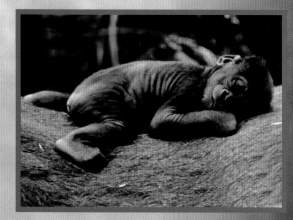

A free ride
This newborn gorilla will cling to its mother's fur for around five months. After that, the baby will ride on its mother's back or shoulders.

Are we there yet?

A gorilla's day

Gorillas spend their mornings
and evenings looking for food
and eating. They spend the
middle part of the day sleeping,
playing, or grooming.

I'm ten months old

I can walk on my own now, but whenever I get tired I hitch a ride with my older brother. I spend most of the day with my brothers and sisters.

Gorillas like to take a nap in the middle of the day.

Sweet dreams

When they go to sleep, gorillas make a nest out of leaves and branches. When they wake up, they eat the leaves and have breakfast in bed.

I also rest with my brothers and sisters.

A baby gibbon

I was born high up in the trees in a tropical rainforest. I live with my mother, my father, and my brothers and sisters. My family spend most of their time high up in the trees.

I can't wait until I'm old enough to swing through the trees.

Gibbons learn to swing through the trees when they are about one year old.

Look how far I can stretch!

Gibbon facts

· ·

Gibbons sleep sitting up.

Gibbons are very good at walking on two feet, just like humans.

Gibbons eat fruit, leaves, and insects, but their favourite food is ripe figs.

Hanging around

My family and I move through the trees by swinging from branch to branch. My long arms and hands help me to hang on to the branches as I move.

Gibbons use their curved hands, feet, and fingers to hook on to branches as they swing from tree to tree.

My brother can swing all the way through

Hanging on with just one hand is easy for a gibbon!

A gibbon
can leap
about 10 m
(30 ft) from
tree to tree.

the forest.

Call of the wild

Each gibbon family makes
up its own songs and sings
them every day. The songs
are very loud and tell other
gibbons to stay away.

Chimpanzee baby

I was born in a forest. I live here with my family and all of our friends. There are always plenty of other chimps for me to play with.

New arrival
The newborn chimp is carried by her mother until she is strong enough to cling to her mother's fur.

Climbing is hard, hanging on is easy.

Chimps eat fruit, insects, honey, flowers, leaves, nuts, and small animals.

Keeping clean

Chimpanzees spend a lot of their time grooming each other. Grooming helps keep the chimps' fur clean and is also a way to make friends.

Baby chimps spend almost all of their time with their mother.

All this fun and play has made me sleepy!

17

Growing and learning

There are so many things to learn before I am all grown up! My sisters and brothers teach me what kinds of food are good to eat. They also show me how to use tools, such as sticks, to reach the food.

Lunch on a stick

Termites are a favourite food for hungry chimps. The termites live in mounds and are hard to reach, so the chimps use a stick to help.

Using tools

Inside the mound the termites crawl up the stick. The chimp pulls it up to get a tasty lunch.

The circle of life goes round and round.

... baby to a gorilla

Now you know how we grew from a ...

... baby to a gibbon

... baby to an orangutan

Bye bye, I'll miss you.

... baby to a chimpanzee

Our ape friends from around the world

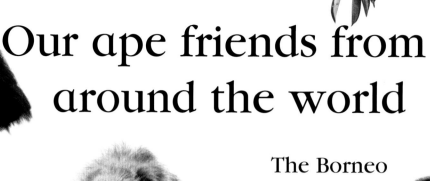

The Borneo gibbon lives only on the tropical island of Borneo.

Siamang apes live in tropical forests in southeast Asia.

The Mountain gorilla lives high up in the mountains in central Africa.

I'm tired!

The Bonobo lives in Africa and is also called the pygmy chimpanzee.

My ape friends live in jungles and forests all around the world.

The Buff-cheeked crested gibbon has yellow or tan fur.

The agile gibbon lives in the tops of jungle trees.

it's time to sleep.

Ape facts

. . . .

Gibbons swing through the trees at about 56 kph (35 mph).

Chimpanzees don't like to be in water and can't swim.

Gorillas live together in groups of about 20, called troops.

The word "orang-utan" means forest person.

23

Glossary

Nest
A place some apes make for sleeping, made out of leaves.

Fur
The soft hair that keeps the ape warm and protects it.

Grooming
When apes use their hands to clean and tidy each other's fur.

Tool
An object used for a special job, like a stick or a rock.

Rainforest
A place with many big trees where it rains a lot.

Troop
A group of animals living together. Chimps live in troops.

Acknowledgements
The publisher would like to thank the following for their kind permission to reproduce their photographs:
(Key: a=above; c=centre; b=below; l=left; r=right; t=top)
1 Alamy: Juniors Bildarchiv. 2-3 Ardea: Kenneth W. Fink. 2 Getty Images: David Allan Brandt c; Catherine Ledner cr. FLPA: Frans Lanting cl. 3 Alamy: Steve Bloom Images. 4 Getty Images: Heinrich van der Berg. 5 Getty Images: Steven Raymer b; Art Wolfe t. 8-9 Getty Images: Tom Brakefield. 8 Ardea: John Cancalosi l. 10 Alamy: Martin Harvey 11 Alamy: Martin Harvey tr, c; NHPA cb. 12 FLPA: Jurgen & Christine Sohns. 13 Ardea London: M. Watson. 14 FLPA: Terry Whittaker tr; NHPA Gerard Lacz l. 15 Corbis: Martin Harvey tl; FLPA: Terry Whittaker r; Getty Images: Manoj Shah bl; NHPA: Martin Harvey tl. 16-17 Corbis: Steven Bein c. 16 Photolibrary: Richard Packwood bl; Steve Bloom Images cl.

17 Photolibrary: Richard Packwood bl; Steve Bloom Images cl. 17 Corbis: Mary Ann McDonald br; Gallo Images tc. 18-19 Getty Images: Digital Vision. 19 Steve Bloom Images r. 20-21 FLPA: Frans Lanting. 20 Alamy: Images of Africa Photobank cr. Ardea London: John Cancalosi c; M. Watson cbr. Corbis: William Manning c. 21 Corbis: Stan Osolinski cr; Lynne Renee cl. Getty Images: Paula Bronstein bl; Gallo Images tl. IPN stock: Catherine Ledner cla. Photolibrary: Stan Osolinski clb. Zefa: T. Allofs cl. 22-23 Alamy: Martin Harvey b. 22 Alamy: Chris Fredriksson tr, David Moore cl. Steve Bloom Images: bl. IPN stock: Catherine Ledner tl. 23 Alamy: Jack Cox-Travel Pics Pro tc. Photolibrary: cr. Steve Bloom Images: tr
All other images © Dorling Kindersley
For further information, see www.dkimages.com